Artists in Their World

Henry Moore

Sally O'Reilly

FRANKLIN WATTS
LONDON•SYDNEY

First published in 2003 by
Franklin Watts
96 Leonard Street,
London EC2A 4XD

Franklin Watts Australia
45-51 Huntley Street
Alexandria,
NSW 2015

© Franklin Watts 2003

Series Editor: Adrian Cole
Editor: Susie Brooks
Series Designer: Mo Choy
Art Director: Jonathan Hair
Picture Researcher: Sue Mennell

A CIP catalogue record for this book
is available from the British Library.

ISBN 0 7496 4660 8

Printed in Hong Kong, China

Acknowledgements

The following biographical images and the work(s) illustrated have been reproduced by kind permission of The Henry
Moore Foundation: The Henry Moore Foundation Archive: 7t, 8, 9t (LH 6), 10t, 11 (LH 43), 17 (LH 59), 18tr, 19t, 27,
30b (LH 339), 32bl (CGM 114), 33, 35 (LH 573), 36b (HMF 3361), 39 (HMF 80 (60)); Courtauld Institute of Art: 20b;
Darren Chung: front cover centre (LH 205), front cover br, 23 (LH 205), 26t; Felix H. Mann: 26t; Michel Muller: 6
(HMF 488), 21 (HMF 1077), 43 (HMF 123), 24b, 37 (LH 627); Fox Photos: 28b; Errol Jackson 26b (LH293), 29 (LH
350), 32t, 32br, 38t; Luke Finn: 13 (LH 58), 31 (LH 344); John Hedgecoe: 34t.
Arcaid/Alex Bartel: 41t © ADAGP, Paris and DACS, London 2003. Bridgeman Art Library/ Lauros/Giraudon: 30t.
Castello Sforzesco, Milan/ Scala Florence: 12b. Didrichsen Art Museum, Helsinki, Finland/Matti Ruotsalainen: 33 ©
Henry Moore Foundation. Ford Motor Company Limited:41b. Geoscience Features Picture Library/RIDA: 12t. ©Jarrold
Publishing/Peter Smith/ with kind permission of the Administrator of Westminster Cathedral: 15b © the Estate of Eric
Gill/ Bridgeman Art Library. Leslie Garland Picture Library: 7b/Paul Ridsdale,40/ Leslie Garland. London Transport
Headquarters, 55, Broadway, London/Bridgeman Art Library: 14 Tate, London 2003,
© The Estate of Jacob Epstein. Courtesy of the Mayor Gallery, London: 18b. Museo Nacional de Antropologia, Mexico
City, Mexico/ Bridgeman Art Library:16t. © Board of Trustees, National Gallery of Art, Washington D.C: 36t/Gift of the
Morris and Gwendolyn Cafritz Foundation. National Gallery, London/Bridgeman Art Library: 16b. Philadelphia Museum
of Art, Pennsylvania, PA/Bridgeman Art Library:38b. Popperfoto: front cover bl, 20t, front cover bc and 24t/Saidman, 25,
28t. Rudolph Staechelin Family Foundation, Basel, Switzerland/Bridgeman Art Library: 9b. Science and Society Picture
Library: 22b. ©Tate, London 2003: 10br © Henry Moore Foundation,19b © Alan Bowness, Hepworth Estate,22 The
Works of Naum Gabo © Nina Williams,24b © Henry Moore Foundation,27 © Henry Moore Foundation,34b © Bruce
McLean. Tate Gallery Archive: 15t. Werner Forman Archive/British Museum 10b.

With special thanks to Emma Stower of The Henry Moore Foundation

Whilst every attempt has been made to clear copyright
should there be any inadvertent omission please apply
in the first instance to the publisher regarding rectification.

Contents

Who was Henry Moore?

Henry Moore was one of the most important sculptors of modern times. He changed the way that people see art by placing huge sculptures outside, in cities or the countryside. His work was criticised at first, but steadily he grew more and more successful. Today, hundreds of Moore's sculptures are on display in parks, squares and major buildings throughout the world.

A VICTORIAN FAMILY

Moore was born in Castleford, Yorkshire in 1898, the seventh in a family of eight brothers and sisters. Their parents, Raymond and Mary, were a strong influence on them all. Raymond was a coalminer who had great ambitions for his children. By the time Henry was born, one brother and two sisters had become teachers – and Henry was expected to do the same.

> *'First become qualified as a teacher like your brothers and sisters have done and then change to art if you wish. Be sure that you have some living in your hand.'*
>
> Raymond Moore

◀ *The Artist's Mother*, 1927, Henry Moore. Mary Moore was a loving mother who worked hard looking after her family at home. She suffered from rheumatism in her back and would ask Moore to massage it. He said that this gave him an early understanding of the gentle curves of the human body.

TIMELINE ▶

30 July 1898	1909	1911	1914	1915	1916	1917	1918
Henry Spencer Moore is born in Castleford, Yorkshire.	Moore learns about Michelangelo and becomes interested in sculpture.	Moore starts pottery classes with art teacher Alice Gostick.	World War I begins.	Moore becomes a student teacher.	Moore teaches in Castleford.	Moore joins the army. Poisoned by gas in France, he returns to England.	Moore becomes an army physical instructor and returns to France just as the war ends.

► Private Moore (front row, far right) with his Civil Service Rifles platoon, 1917.

SCHOOL DAYS

Moore attended his local primary school then won a scholarship to secondary school. He also went to Sunday school, where he discovered the work of Michelangelo (1475-1564) and became interested in sculpture. He was good at art and was determined to make it his career. But at the age of 17, under his father's firm guidance, he began teaching at his old primary school. This was not to last long, however. Moore's teaching career was soon interrupted by World War I.

THE YOUNG SOLDIER

Aged 19, Moore was conscripted into the army and sent to fight. He wrote to his old art teacher, Alice Gostick, about the terrible conditions – the noise, the lack of sleep and how he made drawings of people picking lice from their clothes. During the battle of Cambrai in France, Moore was poisoned by mustard gas and taken back to hospital in England. When he recovered, he spent the rest of the war as a physical training instructor before returning home to Yorkshire in 1919.

▲ Rocky outcrops in the Yorkshire Dales.

THE YORKSHIRE LANDSCAPE

The Yorkshire landscape had a strong effect on Moore. It was a land of contrasts. The countryside boasted rolling hills and large, open skies, while the local mining industry dotted the area with ugly slag heaps. Moore would always remember the shapes of rocky crags, the mountains of coal and the smooth pebbles of the Castleford streets, and they were to appear in his sculptures throughout his life. As he recalled: 'Some things are little on the outside, and rough and common, but I remember the time when the dust and stones of the streets were as precious as gold to my infant eyes.'

Becoming a sculptor

▲ Moore began pottery classes with Alice Gostick while he was still at school, and continued them after the war. This photo, taken in 1919, shows Alice on the far right with Moore on the floor beside her. He said that the lessons 'kept him sane' when he was a teacher.

Moore's art teacher, Alice Gostick, remained an important inspiration to him after the war. When he returned from the army, she encouraged him to pursue his career in art and found out about grants for people whose education had been interrupted by the war.

A CHANCE TO LEARN

With the help of a grant, Moore enrolled at Leeds School of Art. He still lived in Castleford where he attended evening pottery classes, so he had to catch a train to Leeds each day.

After a year of studying drawing at the art school, he announced that he wanted to be a sculptor. Moore was very insistent and so the school set up a sculpture department with him as its only student for the initial year. One of the first people to follow Moore into the department was Barbara Hepworth (1903–75) who was to become his friend and also a famous artist.

TIMELINE ▶

1919	September 1919	1921
Moore returns to Castleford and pottery lessons with Alice Gostick.	Moore enrols at Leeds School of Art. A sculpture department is set up with Moore as the only student. Moore encounters modern art for the first time on a visit to Sir Michael Sadler's collection.	Moore meets fellow student Barbara Hepworth. He wins a scholarship to the Royal Collage of Art in London.

HEADING FOR LONDON

Leeds was just the first step for Moore. In 1921 he won a scholarship to study sculpture at the Royal College of Art in London, where once again he met up with Hepworth. It was during these first years at the college that Moore started to rebel against authority. Most art school training was based on classical and Renaissance art, but Moore wanted to break away from tradition. He refused to use pointing machines to copy classical sculpture, as his teachers insisted, and instead carved directly into stone with a hammer and chisel. 'When I was a student,' he later said, 'direct carving as an occupation, and as a sculptor's natural way of producing things, was simply unheard of.'

◀ *Head of the Virgin*, 1922-23, Henry Moore. This marble piece is a copy of a classical sculpture, but Moore has made it his own by including part of the original block of stone in the composition. It shows both his skill at lifelike carving and his originality in breaking away from tradition.

GLIMPSES OF MODERNISM

In Victorian times, right up to the turn of the 20th century, art in England was still largely academic – it followed traditional teachings from past masters, and had a formal style. Moore had been frustrated by the lack of modern art around him until he met Professor Michael Sadler, the Vice-Chancellor of Leeds University. Sadler had a collection that included paintings by Paul Cézanne (1839-1906), Paul Gauguin (1848-1903), Henri Matisse (1869-1954) and Vincent van Gogh (1853-90). It was Gauguin's work more than anyone else's that opened Moore's eyes to the world beyond Victorian art. In 1891, Gauguin had emigrated to Tahiti in order to make island life the focus of his art.

▶ *When Are You Getting Married?* 1892, Paul Gauguin. Gauguin was one of the first painters to use colour simply as decoration or to create emotion.

Ancient impact

THE BRITISH MUSEUM

Until the British Museum opened in 1759, Britain had no great museum or library at all. The collection originally belonged to Professor Hans Sloane (1660-1753), and consisted of 120,000 specimens, artefacts, prints, drawings, coins and manuscripts. When Sloane died, he left the collection as a gift to the British nation. It was housed in Montagu House, on the current site of the museum, but the building was too small for the growing public interest. In 1823, a new home was designed for it. This 'cathedral to the arts' was Britain's largest public building and took 30 years to complete.

Today many items have been transferred to other museums and galleries, so the British Museum can focus on ancient cultural objects from around the world.

▲ This bronze Benin plaque from early 17th-century Africa is one of many primitive artefacts on display at the British Museum.

◀ This African mask is like many works that Moore saw in the British Museum, although it is actually one he bought for his own collection at a later date. The influence on Moore of this kind of primitive art is clear in his stone *Mask*, 1928 (below right).

In 1921, while studying at the Royal College of Art, Moore discovered Roger Fry's book *Vision and Design* in a library. Reading Fry's essays on ancient art led him to a new fascination – primitive sculpture. From this moment on, Moore spent days in the British Museum drawing ancient sculptures from Egypt, Africa and Mexico.

ABSTRACT FORMS

The term 'primitive' can be used to describe art from many different cultures, but does not include European or Oriental art. Whereas European painting and sculpture tends to be lifelike, primitive figures often have dots for eyes and chunky, tubular limbs. In modern art, this use of exaggerated and simplified forms is called abstraction. Moore recognised that abstraction can be very expressive, and he began to style his work in this way.

TIMELINE ▶

1921	1922	1922/23
Moore discovers Roger Fry's book *Vision and Design* and starts regular visits to the British Museum.	Moore begins carving in stone and wood. He carves his first sculpture of a mother and child. His father dies.	Moore discovers a book on contemporary artist Henri Gaudier-Brzeska (1891-1915) which has a strong influence on his work.

Reclining Woman, 1927
cast concrete 63.5 cm long The Moore Danowski Trust
This simplified figure shows the beginnings of Moore's interest in abstraction.
His reclining figures never had slender limbs or details such as hairs or nails,
as these would have distracted from the impact of the solid forms. In later years,
the heads would often be reduced to shapes without eyes, a nose or a mouth.

*'Fry opened the way to other books and to the realisation of the
British Museum. That was really the beginning.'*

Henry Moore

A taste of Europe

▲ A Portland stone quarry. Moore's *West Wind* (opposite) was carved from Portland stone.

PORTLAND STONE

Portland is an island off the coast of Dorset in the South of England. Quarrying for Portland stone, which is a type of limestone, dates back to the 12th century. However, it only became really popular in the 17th century when Sir Christopher Wren (1632-1723) chose Portland stone for the rebuilding of London after the Great Fire of 1666. John Nash (1752-1835) used it too, for the construction of Buckingham Palace in the 19th century. Today, Portland stone remains a popular material for all types of building, from large business developments to historic restorations and private homes.

In 1922, Moore visited Paris to view the work of the artist Paul Cézanne. He returned to London inspired by what he had seen, and in 1924 he began teaching sculpture at the Royal College of Art (RCA). Teaching supported Moore financially for many years, until he could earn enough from his art.

In 1925 Moore took time off with a scholarship to travel to Paris and Italy. During this trip, he saw works by the Old Masters, including his favourite, Michelangelo.

STYLE DILEMMA

Moore loved the classical work he'd seen in Europe, but he still felt drawn to primitive sculpture. So on returning to London, he battled on in the primitive style and began to exhibit his work. His first solo show was at the Warren Gallery, London, in 1928.

LANDMARK YEAR

The year 1928 was important to Moore for other reasons, too. He met two key people: the art critic Herbert Read (1893-1968), who became a life-long friend and supporter, and a young Russian student, Irina Radetsky – Moore's future wife. He also began his first commission, *West Wind* (opposite), for the London Transport Headquarters.

▶ *Rondanini Pietà*, 1552-64, Michelangelo. Moore greatly admired this piece, saying: 'I don't know of any other single work of art by anyone that is more poignant, more moving.'

TIMELINE ▶

1922	1923	1924	1925	1928
Moore sees Cézanne's work in Paris.	Moore sells his first piece of work as a professional artist.	Moore holds his first exhibition of carvings in London. He becomes sculpture instructor at the Royal College of Art.	He wins a travel scholarship to Italy, then returns to teach at the RCA. He investigates different types of stone at the Geological Society.	Moore has his first solo show at the Warren Gallery, London. He meets Herbert Read and Irina Radetsky. He begins work on *West Wind*.

West Wind, 1928–9

Portland stone 244 cm long London Transport Headquarters, St James's Park Underground Station, London
This sort of one-sided sculpture that comes out slightly from the wall is called a 'relief' sculpture.
Moore's was one of four reliefs carved for this building, which together symbolised the four winds.
The floating movement of his figure's limbs suggests the dynamic power of the weather. Moore decided
that the figure should be female, as the west wind is generally a gentler wind.

*'Sculpture in stone should look honestly like stone...
to make it look like flesh and blood, hair and dimples
is coming down to the level of stage conjurer.'*

Henry Moore

Direct carving

Many sculptors work by making clay models and then casting them in metal. But for much of his career, Moore chose to concentrate on a different method – carving directly into stone or wood.

TRUTH TO MATERIAL

Direct carving was considered risky – one slip of the chisel and the entire piece would be ruined. The phrase 'truth to material' was often used to describe this process because it was as though the artist were working with nature, not against it. Some artists even believed that the sculpture was already in the stone and that they were merely uncovering it.

'I liked the fact that you begin with the block and have to find the sculpture that is inside. You have to overcome the resistance of the material by sheer determination and hard work.'

Henry Moore

In many ways Moore followed the thinking of artist Pablo Picasso (1881-1973) who said that he was not inventing his pictures, but uncovering something that had always existed in the human mind. As he put it: 'I do not seek, I find.'

JACOB EPSTEIN

The sculptor Jacob Epstein (1880-1959), whom Moore admired, also practised direct carving. He was born in New York and began to draw while working in a bronze foundry. In 1902 he went to study art in Paris, where he often visited the Louvre. The ancient and primitive sculpture he saw there was a continuing influence on his work.

◀ *Night*, 1928-9, Jacob Epstein.
This is one of two figures Epstein carved for the same building as Moore's *West Wind* (page 13). They were placed above the doors. But members of the public found Epstein's figures offensive and vandalised them.

HENRI GAUDIER-BRZESKA

Moore was also influenced by a French sculptor who had moved to London in 1911. Gaudier-Brzeska (1891-1915) was considered a young genius but tragically was killed, aged 23, while fighting for the French army.

Moore had first discovered his work while he was a student at the Royal College of Art, and though the two never met, Gaudier-Brzeska inspired Moore to break away from traditional sculptural methods. Gaudier-Brzeska too, admired Epstein, calling him 'the foremost in the small number of good sculptors in Europe'.

◀ The young Henri Gaudier-Brzeska at work on *Head of Ezra Pound*, 1914, using the direct carving technique.

'Sculptural energy is the mountain.'

Henri Gaudier-Brzeska

ERIC GILL

Eric Gill (1882-1940) was a skilled wood engraver, illustrator, sculptor and typeface designer. He produced many carvings for public buildings, including *The Stations of the Cross* in Westminster Cathedral and, alongside Moore, a wind piece for the London Underground Headquarters. But he is perhaps best known internationally for his typeface Gill Sans, which was based on a font designed in 1916 for London Underground signs.

▶ *Stations of the Cross, IV. Jesus Meets His Mother*, 1918, Eric Gill. This is one of a series of reliefs carved for Westminster Cathedral.

BENEDICTA TU IN MULIERIBUS

IV. JESUS MEETS HIS MOTHER

This paragraph is set in Gill Sans. 'Sans' is short for 'sans serif' which means without serif. Serifs are the tiny bars across the end of a letter's stroke in typefaces like the one used for the quotes in this book. Gill Sans is clear and easy to read, and so is known as a 'humanist sans serif'.

Established artist

In 1928, the influential art critic Herbert Read wrote one of the first major articles on Moore's work. It was very supportive and backed up Moore's opinions on truth to material and direct carving.

By now, Moore's sculpture was becoming widely recognised. It was regularly exhibited in London and also began selling abroad. Moore was gaining confidence and themes were developing in his work.

A LIFE-LONG THEME

The one sculpture that impressed Moore more than any other was a limestone carving of the ancient Mexican rain spirit, Chacmool. Moore had seen a picture of it in a German magazine and a plaster cast copy of it in Paris.

Partly thanks to this, the reclining figure became a life-long obsession for Moore. It was both classical and primitive, and it enabled Moore to experiment with shape and explore different ways of sculpting.

▼ **An example of a *Chacmool* from Mexico c.12th century AD. Moore spoke of the Chacmool's 'stillness and alertness, a sense of readiness – and the whole presence of it'.**

RECLINING FIGURES

Reclining figures have a long tradition in art, from primitive and classical sculpture to the paintings of Diego Velázquez (1599-1660), Jean Ingres (1780-1867), Gustave Courbet (1819-77) and Paul Gauguin. During the Renaissance they were used to illustrate the Greek goddess Venus of classical mythology. Later artists used them to explore themes linked to nature. By Moore's time, many Modernist artists were portraying the female nude as strong, powerful and in control.

For sculptors working in stone the reclining nude also has a practical aspect: stone has weak points, and a standing figure might snap off at the ankles or neck.

◄ *Venus at Her Mirror*, 1644-48, Diego Velázquez. Here Venus reclines on her side, spanning the breadth of the canvas.

TIMELINE ▶

May 1929	July 1929	1930
Moore completes his first reclining figure showing clearly the influence of the ancient Mexican rain spirit *Chacmool*. This includes his first use of a hole in his sculpture.	Moore marries Irina. The couple move to Hampstead and become friends with an up-and-coming group of artists.	Moore joins an avant-garde artists' group, *Seven and Five*. He exhibits work in the British Pavilion at the Venice Biennale, an important international art show.

Reclining Figure, 1929

brown Hornton stone 85 cm long Leeds Museums and Galleries

This figure was Moore's first real reference to the Mexican *Chacmool*. It lies at a similar angle, head raised and knees bent, and has the same sense of heaviness. Like the *Chacmool*, too, it confronts the viewer with an inquisitive look. It has a much more striking presence than the *Reclining Woman* Moore carved two years earlier (see page 11). Moore made a great number of female reclining figures, both nude and clad in stone-carved drapery. He only ever sculpted one male reclining figure, and this no longer exists.

'Henry Moore, in virtue of his sureness and consistency, springs straight to the head of the modern movement in England.'

Herbert Read, the Listener magazine, 1928

The Hampstead Set

Moore married Irina Radetsky in 1929, and shortly afterward they moved to Hampstead in northern London. Around the same time, political problems in Europe were driving many artists and writers to London so that it rivaled Paris as the center of the art world.

Hampstead became a base for this creative energy. Moore's neighbors included Barbara Hepworth, Herbert Read, painter Ben Nicholson (1894-1982), and sculptors John Skeaping (1901-80) and Naum Gabo (1890-1977). They went on vacation together and formed artists' groups such as Seven and Five and Unit One. In 1930, Moore was invited to represent British sculpture at the prestigious Venice Biennale along with Jacob Epstein and John Skeaping.

▲ Henry and Irina Moore on their wedding day, July 29, 1929. Moore made many sketches of Irina as they settled into their new life together among the Bohemian intellectuals of Hampstead.

UNIT ONE

The elite, avant-garde artists' group Unit One was established in 1933, and was based at the Mayor Gallery in London. Moore joined the group that year along with painters Paul Nash (1889-1946) and Edward Burra (1905-76), and architect Wells Coates (1895-1958).

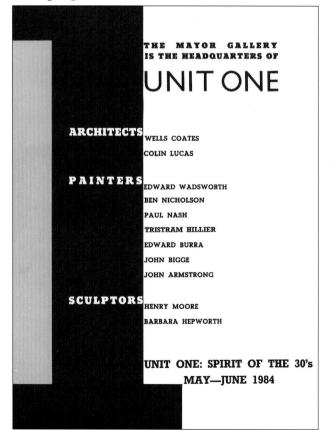

THE MAYOR GALLERY IS THE HEADQUARTERS OF

UNIT ONE

ARCHITECTS WELLS COATES
COLIN LUCAS

PAINTERS EDWARD WADSWORTH
BEN NICHOLSON
PAUL NASH
TRISTRAM HILLIER
EDWARD BURRA
JOHN BIGGE
JOHN ARMSTRONG

SCULPTORS HENRY MOORE
BARBARA HEPWORTH

UNIT ONE: SPIRIT OF THE 30's MAY—JUNE 1984

◀ Catalog from a 1984 exhibition celebrating the work of Unit One. The exhibition was held at the same gallery as the first Unit One exhibition in 1933. The cover is typical of 1930s design which was considered very modern. It reflected the avant-garde nature of the group.

The Unit One artists announced in *The Times* that they promoted "the expression of a truly contemporary spirit" – in other words, creating art and architecture with a very up-to-date feel. In 1933, to coincide with the publication of Read's book *Art Now*, the Mayor gallery held an exhibition with works by Unit One artists Moore, Hepworth, Nicholson, along with distinguished European artists.

▲ On vacation at Happisburgh, Norfolk, England, 1931. From left to right: artist Ivon Hitchens (1893-1979), Irina Moore, Henry Moore, Barbara Hepworth, Ben Nicholson, and friend Mary Jenkins.

BARBARA HEPWORTH

Like Moore, Barbara Hepworth (1903-75) was born in Yorkshire, England, and studied at the Leeds School of Art and the Royal College of Art in London. While living in Hampstead she developed a strong working relationship with Moore. Their sculptures show many similarities. They were once overheard arguing over which of them was copying the other! They shared an interest in landscape, abstraction, truth to material, and direct carving, but Hepworth's work is considered more serene and classical than Moore's.

Hepworth was married to Ben Nicholson, and together they traveled around Europe visiting important abstract artists. Barbara received many public commissions and awards throughout her career, including the Grand Prix at the São Paulo Biennale in 1959, and Dame Commander of the British Empire in 1965. She died in a house fire in 1975.

▲ *Mother and Child*, 1934, Barbara Hepworth.
The similarities to Moore's abstract work are clear to see, but overall Hepworth's sculpture is more delicate.

The Surreal Thirties

▲ Government militia fight in the streets of Barcelona during the Spanish Civil War, 1936.

THE SPANISH CIVIL WAR

In 1936 civil war broke out in Spain. An extreme right-wing group called the Fascists were fighting viciously for control of the country, and three years later they finally declared victory. Fascist General Franco was made Spain's head of state, and he remained leader, or dictator, until his death in 1975.

Many artists and writers wanted to fight against the Fascists. Some actually fought, such as the writer George Orwell (1903-50), while others, such as Ernest Hemingway (1899-1961) and W.H. Auden (1907-73), drove ambulances or helped in other ways. Moore signed the manifesto of the English Surrealist Group against British non-intervention in Spain and tried to go there, but his request for a travel permit was rejected.

In 1931 Moore resigned from the Royal College of Art after a newspaper article about his work caused a public scandal. But it was only a brief setback. Soon afterwards Moore was employed to start up a sculpture department at Chelsea College of Art.

SURREALISM

In London at this time, artists were becoming interested in a movement called Surrealism that had begun in Europe in the early 1920s. Surrealists, such as Salvador Dalí (1904-89), based their art on images from the unconscious mind and dreams. As a result, it was often irrational – hard to make sense of.

Although Moore agreed with some of the Surrealists' ideas, he was never entirely associated with them. He would pick and choose aspects of the movement, such as imagination and inventiveness, but preferred to control how his sculpture looked instead of letting his subconscious mind take over.

▲ Photograph of the International Surrealist Exhibition at the New Burlington Galleries, London, 1936. Moore showed work at this event including *Reclining Figure*, 1933 (centre stand) and *Figure*, 1933-34 (far right stand).

TIMELINE ▶

1932	1933	1934	1935	1936
Moore is appointed head of the new sculpture department at Chelsea College of Art.	Moore joins avant-garde group *Unit One*.	The Moores make a trip to Spain, visiting Barcelona, Madrid, Toledo and Altamira.	Moore has an exhibition of drawings at the Zwemmer Gallery, London.	The Spanish Civil War breaks out. Moore signs the manifesto of the English Surrealist Group against British non-intervention in Spain.

Two Seated Women, 1934

charcoal, watercolour, pen and ink, crayon on cream medium-weight wove paper
37 x 55 cm The Henry Moore Foundation, Perry Green
Moore's inventiveness with the human form was close to that of the Surrealists.
They created images that would not be seen in reality. In this drawing, Moore distorts
the human figures into fantastic shapes so that they are part biology, part geometry.

'There are universal shapes to which everybody is subconsciously
conditioned and to which they can respond if their conscious
mind does not shut them off.'

Henry Moore

Abstract Forms

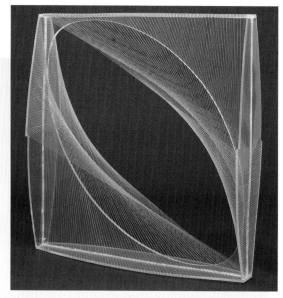

▲ *Linear Construction No. 1, 1942-43, Naum Gabo.* From his initial sketches, Gabo constructed many stringed sculptures such as this one.

THE ART OF CONSTRUCTION

Other artists also worked from scientific and mathematical models. Hepworth had started to experiment with stringed sculpture around the same time, and the Russian artist Naum Gabo (1890-1977) – now also living in Hampstead – made drawings of stringed objects as early as 1933. In Russia in 1920, Gabo and his brother Antoine Pevsner (1886-1962) had issued a "constructivist manifesto." They aimed to move away from traditional sculptural methods, such as stone carving, and to explore space with new forms and materials. They wanted to create a classless society that used architecture and technology to make everyone equal.

While Moore was experimenting with Surrealist ideas, he was also developing his abstract style. During the 1930s his work became increasingly simplified and removed from reality. Moore insisted that it was as true to nature as lifelike art. He was simply reducing objects to their simplest form, or building them up from basic shapes.

STRINGED SCULPTURE

On a visit to London's Science Museum, Moore came across mathematical models that used string or nylon to create a line. When he incorporated these lines into his sculptures, they opened up his blocky forms allowing light through. Moore was excited by "the ability to look through the strings as with a bird cage and to see one form within another."

"There is just as much shape in a hole as a lump."

Henry Moore

◄ **An example of a mathematical model from the Science Museum in London.**

TIMELINE ▶

1937	1938	1939	1940
Moore visits Picasso's studio in Paris to see the famous painting *Guernica*. He produces his first stringed sculpture.	Moore is refused a permit to visit Spain. He starts to use modeling and casting as well as direct carving. He participates in the International Exhibition of Abstract Art at the Stedelijk Museum in Amsterdam.	Moore resigns from the Chelsea College of Art. World War II begins.	Moore takes over Hepworth's studio in Hampstead.

Bird Basket, 1939

lignum vitae and string, 16 ¹/₂ in (42 cm) long, The Henry Moore Foundation, Perry Green, England

Moore wrote, "It is called the *Bird Basket* because it has the handle of a basket over the top and strings to show the little inner piece as a bird inside a cage – at one end is the head and at the other the tail." Moore uses string just as a painter would use a brush to paint a line. The line stands out against the solid form of the wood and emphasizes the three-dimensional space.

"They think that abstraction means getting away from reality and it often means precisely the opposite – that you are getting closer to it… nearer to an emotional understanding."

Henry Moore

War artist

While Moore was growing steadily more successful, Europe was spiralling into full-scale war. At 11.15 am on Sunday 3 September 1939, the British Prime Minister Neville Chamberlain announced that Britain was at war with Germany.

Moore had fought in World War I, but was now too old to be conscripted into the army. Initially he turned down an invitation to be an official war artist, thinking he could be more useful as a precision tool maker – but then events around him persuaded him to change his mind. During the months of waiting for a training place, he made drawings of people taking shelter from the air raids in London. The official bomb shelters were not big enough, so people carried rolled-up bedding and took cover on the platforms of underground stations.

▲ Moore revisited the London Underground in September 1943 to film *Out of Chaos*, a documentary about war artists which also included Paul Nash and Stanley Spencer.

'I saw people lying on the platforms at all the stations we stopped at… I had never seen so many reclining figures, and even the train tunnels seemed to be like the holes in my sculpture.'

Henry Moore

◀ *Tube Shelter Perspective: The Liverpool Street Extension*, 1941, Henry Moore. The scratchy effect comes from using pen, chalk and paint together. It gives the drawing a ghostly, anxious feel, reflecting the mood in the shelters during air raids.

AN OFFICIAL SCHEME

The official war artists scheme was first set up by the government during World War I. It began in 1916, mainly as a means of getting messages to the public, but it soon became an important way of recording events in the war, too. Many great artists were involved, including painters Paul Nash (1889-1946), John Singer Sargent (1856-1925) and Stanley Spencer (1891-1959). On the outbreak of World War II the War Artists' Advisory Committee began to commission artists in a similar way.

> *'It seemed a good way of preventing artists being killed.'*
>
> *Kenneth Clark, War Artists' Advisory Committee*

MOORE FOR MORALE

When the Committee saw Moore's shelter drawings, they immediately asked him to record the Blitz in London. The work would be exhibited around the country to boost morale. Moore changed his mind and became an official war artist, earning enough to survive without teaching for the first time.

THE UNDERGROUND ARMY

In 1942 Moore began another drawing project that linked his job as war artist with his upbringing in Yorkshire. He returned to Castleford to sketch the coal miners, known as the Underground Army. Moore found this hard. He preferred to draw the female form, and found the harsh movements of the pit men too different from his usual still subjects.

THE LONDON BLITZ

In 1940 the German air force bombed British airfields and radar stations, in preparation for the invasion of England. The invasion never happened, but instead Hitler ordered the destruction of London by air raids. On 7 September 1940, German planes bombed the capital for 12 hours. This intense attack, known as the Blitz, continued for months. Whole areas of London were destroyed. The Blitz ended on 11 May 1941, when Hitler called off the raids in order to move his bombers east and invade Russia.

The Blitz affected Moore directly. In 1940 a bomb fell close to his home in Hampstead, destroying the doors and windows. Soon afterwards, another blast cut off the gas and water supplies. The Moores decided to leave the city and move to a farmhouse called Hoglands in Perry Green, Hertfordshire. This was a turning point for Moore, who saw his work in the open countryside for the first time.

▲ Families trying to recover from the devastation of their homes after the Blitz, London, 1940-41.

Family and Fame

FESTIVAL OF BRITAIN

The Festival of Britain took place between May and September of 1951. After the hardship of the war years, the Festival's goal was to raise the nation's spirits and promote British art, design, and industry. Moore created a reclining figure especially for the event. The South Bank Exhibition and the Festival Pleasure Gardens in Battersea were the main London venues, but there were celebrations all over Britain. People still affected by shortages and rationing due to the war were offered fun and education with theater, dance, music, art exhibitions, firework displays, cafés, and entertaining sideshows. Post-war freedom was to be enjoyed by everyone.

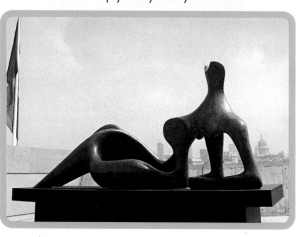

▲ *Reclining Figure: Festival*, 1951, on display at London's South Bank. This was one of the first pieces in which Moore tried to make the gaps and spaces as important as the bronze itself. The figure is almost half air.

World War II finally ended in 1945, and Europe started rebuilding from the devastation. Families were reunited and desperately wanted to return to normalcy.

On March 7, 1946, Moore's only child, Mary, was born. Britain was being reborn, which led to the commissioning of large public sculptures in new towns throughout southern England. One of these was Moore's *Family Group* (opposite).

▲ **Moore at home with his daughter Mary, Easter 1951.**

BRANCHING OUT

By now Moore was realizing that the idea of "truth to material" could also be applied to bronze. He could do things with bronze that he couldn't do with stone. He could cast upright figures without the sculpture breaking in two. Bronze would also last better outdoors.

This new development coincided with Moore's growing international success. In 1943, he had his first solo exhibition abroad – in New York. This was followed by a traveling retrospective which opened in 1946. In 1948, Moore represented Britain at the Venice Biennale and won the International Prize for Sculpture for his one-man show.

TIMELINE ▶

1944	1945	1946	1948	1949	1951
Moore's mother dies.	World War II ends.	Birth of Moore's only child, Mary.	Moore has a solo show at the Venice Biennale. He wins the International Prize for Sculpture.	Moore holds an exhibition at the Palais des Beaux-Arts, Brussels, which then travels (1948-51) to Paris, Amsterdam, Hamburg, Düsseldorf, Berne, and Athens.	Moore visits Greece and its classical ruins. He participates in the Festival of Britain and has a retrospective at the Tate Gallery.

Family Group, 1948–49

bronze, 59 in (152 cm) high, Tate, London, England

Moore sculpted many family groups which were just right for the optimistic atmosphere that developed in England after the war. They symbolized unity and hope for the future.

Royal recognition

By the 1950s Moore was recognised worldwide as an influential figure. He was offered a knighthood by King George VI in 1950, but refused as he felt it might cut him off from his fellow artists.

Gone were the days when Moore had caused outrage with his modern approach and ideas. Now his work was universally accepted and he became a respected member of established art societies.

TO SCOTLAND

Moore had many wealthy supporters, one of which was the businessman Sir William Keswick. On a visit to Moore's house, Keswick saw a large bronze on the lawn and decided that he wanted it for his own estate at Glenkiln in Scotland. So *King and Queen* (opposite) was placed on a rock on the bleak moor.

> *'It's a most glorious place for it, very wild and surprisingly right.'*
>
> Henry Moore

▲ Queen Elizabeth II at her coronation, 1953.

▲ Moore (seated fourth from the right) with other members of the Order of Merit at Buckingham Palace, 1972.

THE CORONATION

It is likely that Moore's idea for *King and Queen* stemmed from the excitement leading up to the coronation of Elizabeth II. Elizabeth was crowned Queen on 2 June 1953, following the death of her father George VI in February 1952.

The build-up to the ceremony was very public, and it was the first royal event to be televised. Some thought that this was undignified, but an estimated 20 million people saw the young Queen crowned.

Moore was later to meet Elizabeth in person. In 1955 she made him a Companion of Honour, and in 1963 awarded him the Order of Merit.

TIMELINE ▶

1952	1953	1954	1955
Moore has exhibitions in Sweden, South Africa, Austria and the Netherlands.	Moore is awarded the International Sculpture Prize at the second São Paulo Biennale. He travels to Brazil and Mexico.	Moore's international reputation continues to grow.	Moore is made a Companion of Honour by Queen Elizabeth II. He becomes a Trustee of the National Gallery.

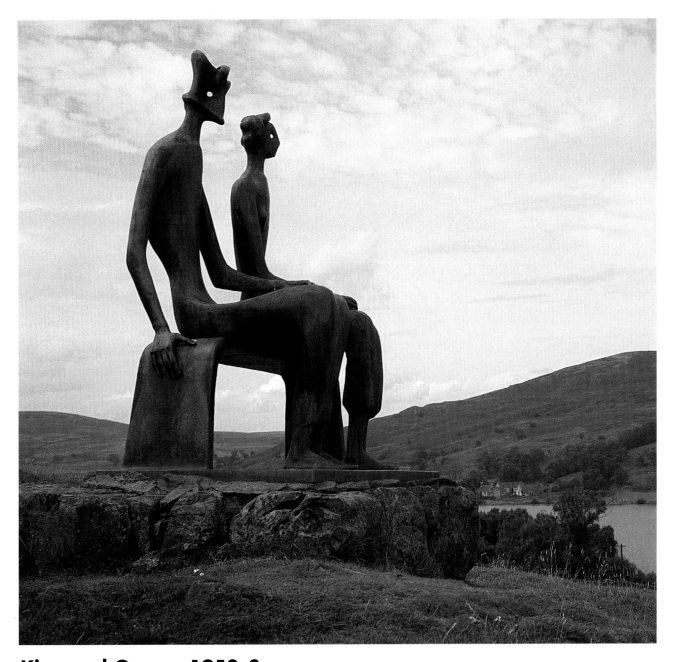

King and Queen, 1952–3
bronze 164 x 138 x 84.5 cm Keswick Estate, Glenkiln, Dumfriesshire, Scotland
The two figures in this sculpture are an odd couple, sitting serenely in the Scottish
countryside. They stare out over the water of the loch in a regal and dignified pose.

*'I was reading stories to Mary, my six-year-old daughter,
every night, and most of them were about kings and
queens and princesses.'*

Henry Moore

Giant Commissions

▲ Gargoyles high up on the walls of Notre Dame Cathedral stare down on the city of Paris far below them.

SCULPTURE TO LOOK UP TO

There have been sculptures around the tops of buildings for centuries. In medieval times builders made gargoyles, which were often ornamental spouts designed to carry rainwater away from roofs.

Gargoyles were carved to look like animals or human faces. They can still be seen today on many churches. Moore had made copies of gargoyles in Leeds while he was a student.

There are many myths about gargoyles. They are supposed to stand guard and ward off unwanted spirits and other creatures, or come alive at night when everyone's asleep and protect the church. Winged gargoyles are said to fly round the village or town and return to their places when the sun comes up.

During the 1950s Moore started receiving large commissions from big businesses. He could now impress the public more than ever. His success enabled him to hire assistants – young sculptors such as Anthony Caro (b.1924) – to help him.

THE TIME-LIFE SCREEN

A new building on Bond Street in London had just been built for the *Time-Life Magazine* company. Its owners wanted it to reflect British creative talent so they invited Moore to contribute.

Moore installed one of his reclining figures in the third floor garden terrace and then created a huge screen that went around the top of the building. He planned this large sculpture – and almost all sculptures after that – using small scale models called maquettes.

▲ *Time-Life Screen: Maquette No.1*, 1952, Henry Moore. Maquettes are like 3-D sketches. They enabled Moore to plan large sculptures without having to work with large pieces. His assistants would help enlarge the final maquettes. Moore said, "Always in my mind, though, in making these little ideas, is the eventual sculpture which may be ten or twelve times the size of the maquette that I hold in my hand."

TIMELINE ▶

1957	1959	1960
Moore shows work at the fourth International Exhibition of Sculpture in the Open Air in London.	Moore receives more awards and has many exhibitions worldwide.	Many German towns commission large bronzes by Moore as public sculptures. Alice Gostick, Moore's pottery teacher, dies.

Time-Life Screen, 1952-53

Portland stone, 318 $^1/_9$ in (808 cm) long, Pearl Assurance, Time-Life Building, London, England

Moore wanted the four large sculptures to be on a turntable so that they could be rotated each month, but that was too dangerous. Instead, he made the carvings three dimensional so that the overall effect was of figures embedded in the screens. There were holes incorporated into the design so that the passer-by could see it was sculpture and not part of the building.

"There is a right physical size for every idea."

Henry Moore

A collector of objects

▲ Moore's collection of objects in the sitting room at Hoglands, 1966.

ETCHING TECHNIQUE

The technique of etching is a painstaking process. The artist scratches a picture onto a highly polished sheet of copper which has been coated with an acid resistant substance, known as 'ground'. The copper is then immersed in a bath of acid which 'bites' into the scratched lines. Next it is covered with ink, then cleaned to leave ink in the grooves only. The plate is then placed on an etching press and covered with a sheet of heavy, damp paper. The press forces the paper into the ink-filled grooves and the image is transferred onto the paper.

During his lifetime, Moore collected many objects and artworks. The sitting room at Hoglands was full of ancient sculpture, curios, bones and stones as well as 19th-century paintings. Works by his British contemporaries, such as Paul Nash and Ben Nicholson, were elsewhere in the house.

SKULLS AND BONES

It would be hard for us to tell the difference between the natural and the man-made things in Moore's collection. But for him every piece had a meaning, in particular an elephant skull he had been given. Not only did this inspire the sculpture *Atom Piece*, but it also led Moore to take up etching.

▲ *Elephant Skull Plate I*, 1969. Moore's etched lines follow the curving, 3-D form of the skull.

▲ Moore working on an etching plate with the elephant skull in his studio at Hoglands, 1970.

TIMELINE ▶

1961	1963	1964
Moore is elected a member of the American Academy of Art and Letters. He exhibits at the Scottish National Gallery of Modern Art, Edinburgh.	Moore takes up etching. He receives the Order of Merit from Queen Elizabeth II.	Moore is appointed a member of the Arts Council of Great Britain and reappointed as a Trustee of the National Gallery.

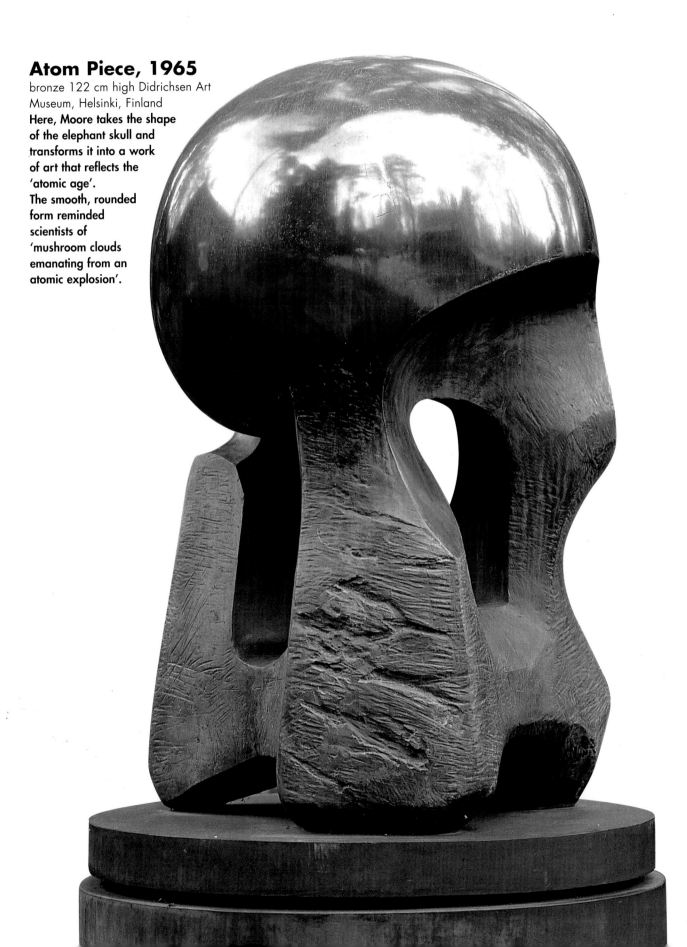

Atom Piece, 1965

bronze 122 cm high Didrichsen Art
Museum, Helsinki, Finland
**Here, Moore takes the shape
of the elephant skull and
transforms it into a work
of art that reflects the
'atomic age'.
The smooth, rounded
form reminded
scientists of
'mushroom clouds
emanating from an
atomic explosion'.**

33

Marble marvels

THE CHANGING ART WORLD

In 1968, the Tate Gallery, London, held a retrospective of Moore's work. This was a time when youth culture was on the rise, students were rebelling and there were student riots in many countries. Moore's old assistant Anthony Caro was now rivalling the popularity of his master. It was a decade of experimental sculpture and conceptual art, which meant that a thought often counted for more than an object. An artwork could be a walk through the countryside or a sentence on a wall. One artist, Bruce McLean (b.1944), exhibited photographs of himself pretending to be Moore's reclining figures.

▲ *Pose Work for Plinths 3*, 1971, Bruce Mclean. McLean was pointing out that art was no longer just about sculpture and painting.

In 1965, Moore bought a house near the Carrara marble quarries in Italy. From here, he could easily access the marble and work on his large public sculptures nearby. Moore was increasingly interested in marble and its potential for creating smooth, curvaceous forms. It also gave him a link to the great classical sculptors he so admired. Michelangelo had used the same source of marble for his own work.

▲ Moore at the Henraux marble quarry in the Carrara Mountains, Italy, not far from his villa. Moore would spend summer mornings working here, as the marble slabs were too heavy to take to his studio.

MOTHER AND CHILD

Mother and Child is an example of how Moore used the natural qualities of marble to make his work expressive. Here, the red veins in the stone run between the two figures, giving them life and suggesting a bond between them. At the same time, the polished curves remind us of the softness of the human body. Throughout his career, Moore was obsessed with the 'Mother and Child' theme. Among other things, it reflected the subject matter of many paintings and sculptures by the Old Masters.

TIMELINE ▶

1965	1967	1968
Moore buys a summer house in Italy. He also visits New York for the installation of a *Reclining Figure* at the Lincoln Center.	Replicas of Moore's work are used in a set for the opera *Don Giovanni* in Italy. Moore visits Canada. He is elected Fellow of the British Academy.	Moore has a retrospective at the Tate Gallery, to coincide with his 70th birthday. He is created Honorary Doctor by the Royal College of Art, London.

Mother and Child, 1967

rosa aurora marble 130.8 cm long The Henry Moore Foundation, Perry Green

Moore is considered a 'humanist' artist because he dealt with familiar themes that we have all experienced. In this piece, he portrays the relationship between mother and child in an abstract way – the large form in contact with the small form gives a feeling of protection. Perhaps Moore was inspired by the relationship he had with his own mother.

'It has been a universal theme from the beginning of time ... I discovered, when drawing, I could turn every little scribble, blot or smudge into a Mother and Child.'

Henry Moore

Home and away

▲ *Knife Edge Mirror Two-Piece*, 1977-8, stands outside the National Gallery of Art in Washington DC. Moore made this bronze piece enormous (nearly 8 metres high) so that from a distance it didn't look like a person going into the gallery.

CASTING IN BRONZE

There are two main methods of bronze casting: 'sand casting' and 'lost wax casting'. Moore used wax, and for a while he did it himself with the help of two assistants. Most of the time though, he had his casting done at professional foundries.

In the lost wax method, a wax replica is made of the artist's original work (which is usually a plaster or clay model). This replica is covered with 'grog' – a mixture of water, plaster and ground-up pottery – which sets hard around the wax. The mould is then baked in a kiln. The heat melts the wax which runs out of a hole left in the mould. Molten bronze is poured in through the hole so that it fills the space left by the 'lost' wax. The final piece is then hand-finished to smooth off any rough areas.

By the time Moore reached his 70s, his art was on display all over the world. But his age did not limit his travelling or the size of his sculptures at all. In between trips abroad, Moore kept up work at Hoglands.

SCALE AND STATURE

Moore had separate studios for different ways of working, including maquettes, printmaking and a huge outdoor studio for large sculpture. By this stage in his life, he was wealthy enough to be extravagant with scale and material, and most of his later works were massive monuments cast in bronze.

Sheep Piece (opposite) was one of these. Moore had started drawing sheep during preparations for a big exhibition in Florence in 1972. There were so many people packing up his work that he retreated to a room facing fields where his neighbour's sheep grazed. They wandered up close to the window and, fascinated, Moore began to draw them.

◄ *Head*, 1972, page 45 from *Sheep Sketchbook*, Henry Moore. Moore kept a sketchbook of his many sheep drawings.

TIMELINE ▶

1972	1974	1975	1976
The Henry Moore Trust is set up. Moore receives more honours and holds more major exhibitions, including a large retrospective in Florence, Italy.	The Henry Moore Sculpture Centre is opened in Ontario, Canada.	Barbara Hepworth dies in a fire.	There is an exhibition of war drawings at the Imperial War Museum, including a selection by Moore.

Sheep Piece, 1971-2

bronze 550 cm tall The Henry Moore Foundation, Perry Green

Moore placed many of his sculptures in the countryside because he thought the open sky made a dramatic background. *Sheep Piece* was made to stand in a field where his neighbours' lambs could play around it. It became a shelter for the sheep and also served as a back rub. Moore preferred his sculpture to be among sheep rather than cows or horses, as their small size enhanced the impressive scale of his work.

'At first I saw them as rather shapeless balls of wool with a head and four legs. Then I began to realise that underneath all that wool was a body, which moved in its own way, and that each sheep had its individual character.'

Henry Moore

The last years

Moore had an extremely long and successful career as an artist, and outlived many of his friends. He had become a grandfather, travelled the globe and received many awards. He had always been ambitious and seemed to have followed the very best path for a world renowned sculptor.

By the end of his life, Moore's work was visible in many parts of the world and he had dozens of public sculptures in the United States alone.

FINAL FEATS

In his later years, Moore suffered from arthritis and general ill health, and so naturally he became less productive. Nevertheless, work still went on at Hoglands. Moore had kept many old maquettes from previous decades, and throughout the 1980s his assistants made new casts from these. Moore continued to draw meanwhile, and his work still made its mark elsewhere. In 1982 the Henry Moore Centre for the Study of Sculpture opened in Leeds.

▲ Towards the end of his life Moore spent much of his time drawing at home.

Moore died on 31 August 1986 at the age of 88. A memorial service was held at Westminster Abbey, London. His wife, Irina, died two years later.

CÉZANNE'S BATHERS

A favourite theme for Moore's late drawings was Paul Cézanne's paintings of bathers. Cézanne was said to be a forerunner of an art style called Cubism because he reduced nature to basic geometric shapes. He also began to use colours to create different moods.

Moore had first seen Cézanne's *Bathers* in Paris when he was a student. There is a noticeable similarity between Cézanne's paintings of curvaceous bodies and Moore's drawn and sculpted figures.

◄ *Large Bathers*, 1899-1906, Paul Cézanne. Cézanne disorted natural forms to suit his own artistic purpose.

TIMELINE ▶

1977	1979	1982	31 August 1986
The Henry Moore Foundation is established in Perry Green. Moore's grandson Gus is born.	Moore's 'Mother and Child' theme becomes dominant. He gets arthritis and has to start working on a smaller scale.	Henry Moore Centre for the Study of Sculpture opens in Leeds. A *Reclining Figure* that Moore carved from elmwood in 1946 sells for $1,000,000 at an auction in New York.	Henry Moore dies.

Study After Cézanne's 'Bathers', 1980

carbon line, wax crayon, watercolour, chalk, chinagraph on heavyweight wove paper 25 x 13.7 cm
The Henry Moore Foundation, Perry Green
Moore's drawings have the same solidity as his monumental sculptures. It is as though he has turned
Cézanne's painted figures into a drawing of stone carvings. Neither Cézanne nor Moore was interested
in portraying the human body in perfect proportion. Their figures have a life of their own which comes
from the sensitive and energetic use of the artist's chosen material.

'I find in all the artists that I admire most a disturbing element,
a distortion, giving evidence of a struggle… In great art, this
conflict is hidden, it is unresolved. All that is bursting with
energy is disturbing – not perfect.'

Henry Moore

Moore's legacy

Moore had a profound effect on the way sculpture is presented to the public today. One of the most revolutionary things about him was his desire to place work out in the open. Most artists preferred to show art in galleries, where attention was focused on it. Sculpture outside the gallery tended to be limited to historical monuments of famous generals or politicians. Moore changed all this, and he had financial backing.

During the 1980s, more companies and governments around the world invested in public art and sculpture. These works of art are now popular landmarks in the towns and cities of many countries.

FIGURES IN LANDSCAPE

A large number of artists have been influenced by Moore's work with the figure in landscape. They include Antony Gormley (b.1950), whose *Angel of the North*, in north-east England, stands 20 metres tall with a wingspan of 52 metres. Towering against the sky, it can be seen for miles around and its roadside position is passed by some 90,000 vehicles every day. Most of the £800,000 this public sculpture cost was provided by the UK National Lottery.

'The hilltop site is important and has the feeling of being a megalithic mound.'

Antony Gormley

◀ *Angel of the North*, 1998, Antony Gormley. This striking figure stands on the remains of an old mine in north-east England. It is a powerful symbol of humanity and the achievements of the industrial age. As Gormley put it: 'When you think of the mining that was done underneath the site, there is a poetic resonance. Men worked beneath the surface in the dark. Now, in the light, there is a celebration of this industry.'

CITY SCULPTURE

French artist Niki de Saint Phalle (1930-2002) made brightly coloured, oversized figures for cityscapes and sculpture gardens. She famously collaborated with the Swiss artist Jean Tinguely (1925-91) to create a landmark fountain for the plaza of the Pompidou Centre in Paris.

> *'Life… is never the way one imagines it.'*
>
> *Niki de Saint Phalle*

▲ *Igor Stravinsky Fountain*, completed 1983, Niki de Saint Phalle and Jean Tinguely. This fountain stands outside the Pompidou Centre, Paris. Inspired by the music of composer Igor Stravinsky, the fun rotating figures contrast brilliantly with the serious industrial look of the building.

THE HENRY MOORE FOUNDATION

Moore established The Henry Moore Foundation at Perry Green in 1977, in order to 'advance the education of the public by the promotion of their appreciation of the fine arts', and in particular the works of Henry Moore. The Foundation runs the Henry Moore Institute in Leeds, collaborates with artists and galleries to show new work, and awards grants in support of artists' projects. It also owns the largest collection of Moore's work, much of which is displayed in the buildings and grounds of the artist's estate.

BIOMORPHIC DESIGN

▼ The Ford KA was first introduced in 1996. It is an example of modern biomorphic design.

In the 1950s, when Moore was at his creative height, product design echoed the forms of nature. Household objects had curved corners, tables were shaped like kidneys and fabric patterns were made up of abstract leaf or atom shapes. Designers from the period took some of their ideas from artists such as Moore, Hepworth and Nicholson, who looked to nature for inspiration. Now, in the 21st century, this look has been revived. Cars, computers and running shoes are more curvaceous and organic looking than previously. Technology is using nature to solve problems such as wind resistance and fuel efficiency or to make things more user-friendly.

The writings of Henry Moore

In his notebooks and published essays, Moore kept a thorough record of his development as an artist. He had strong opinions on his own work and the work of others, as well as on sculpture in general.

LOOK BEYOND NATURE

One of Moore's main aims was to avoid the tradition of realistic sculpture. Classical statues tried to make stone and marble look like the person they were portraying. He thought that stone should look like stone and that nature should not just be copied.

'The first hole in a piece of stone is a revelation. The hole connects one side to the other, making it immediately more three-dimensional.'

◄ Moore also understood the importance of 'negative space' or the holes around and within a sculpture.

► Moore was more concerned about working in a way that was right for the piece than he was about following a specific art style.

'...inspiration will come, as always, from nature and the world around him, from which he learns such principles as balance, rhythm, organic growth of life, attraction and repulsion, harmony and contrast... but mechanical copying of objects and surrounding life will leave him dissatisfied.'

▲ Moore makes it clear what he understands the role of an artist to be – to use nature as a springboard but not to imitate it directly.

ART CAN BE ABSTRACT AND SURREAL

There was a lot of debate about which was more important, Abstraction or Surrealism. Moore's work contained elements of both. He sometimes began a drawing of abstract shapes – with no particular idea in mind, which is a Surrealist way of working.

'All good art has contained both abstract and surreal elements... order and surprise, intellect and imagination, conscious and unconscious. Both sides of the artist's personality must play their part.'

TIMELINE ►

1898	1918	1922	1928	1937
30 July 1898 Henry Spencer Moore is born in Castleford, Yorkshire.	**1918** Becomes army physical instructor. Returns to France just as war ends.	**1922** Begins carving in stone and wood. Visits Paris, where he sees Cézanne's work.	**1928** First solo show in London. Meets Herbert Read and Irina Radetsky.	**1937** Visits Picasso's studio in Paris. Produces his first stringed sculpture.
1911 Starts pottery classes with Alice Gostick.	**1919** Returns to Castleford.	**1923** Sells first piece of work as professional artist.	**1929** Marries Irina. They move to Hampstead.	**1938** Starts to use casting rather than direct carving.
1914 World War I begins.	**1920** Wins scholarship to Leeds School of Art. Moore is only sculpture student.	**1924** First exhibition of carvings in London. Starts work as sculpture instructor at Royal College of Art.	**1930** Joins *Seven and Five* society. Exhibits at Venice Biennale.	**1939** World War II breaks out. Moore resigns from Chelsea College of Art.
1915 Leaves school to become a student teacher.	**1921** Meets Barbara Hepworth. Wins scholarship to London's Royal College of Art. Discovers book *Vision and Design* and the British Museum.	**1925** Departs on travel scholarship to Italy.	**1932** Appointed head of sculpture at Chelsea College of Art.	**1940** Moves to Perry Green.
1916 Works as a teacher.			**1933** Joins *Unit One*.	**1945** End of World War II.
1917 Joins the army. Is poisoned by mustard gas and returns to England.				**1946** Moore's only child, Mary, is born.

SIZE MATTERS

Moore was very sure about how he wanted a sculpture to appear in the landscape. The size of a piece was very important to him. He also made links between the landscape, the human body and the material that he worked with.

> 'My own scale? It's just over life size. I think that's because I want my work to stand out-of-doors and be seen in a natural setting, and figures seen out of doors always look slightly smaller than they are.'

▲ Moore didn't want his work to be dwarfed by nature, but to complement it.

> 'Besides the human form, I am tremendously excited by all natural forms, such as cloud formations, birds, trees and their roots, and mountains, which are to me the wrinkling of the earth's surface, like drapery. It is extraordinary how closely ripples in the sand on the seashore resemble the gouge marks in wood carving.'

◀ This quote from Moore about natural forms helps to explain the concept of 'truth to material'.

HENRY MOORE'S NOTEBOOKS

Moore wrote hundreds of pages of notes and essays about art, as well as producing nearly 1,200 sculptures and at least 5,500 drawings. It helped that he spent time with other artists and intellectuals and was used to talking about his work and ideas.

Throughout his career he kept detailed notebooks charting his thoughts and progress. His notes and drawings of artefacts in the British Museum, for example, provide the most thorough account of primitive art by any modern artist. But although Moore wrote more than most artists, it was only ever to help his artwork.

◀ *Studies of Sculpture from the British Museum* page 105, Notebook No.3, 1922-24.

1948	1955	1961	1968	1979
1948 Has solo show at Venice Biennale and wins International Prize for Sculpture.	**1955** Made a Companion of Honour by Queen Elizabeth II. Becomes a Trustee of the National Gallery.	**1961** Elected member of American Academy of Art and Letters.	**1968** Retrospective at the Tate Gallery.	**1979** Develops arthritis and has to work on a smaller scale.
1951 Visits Greece and its classical ruins. Participates in Festival of Britain and has his first retrospective at the Tate Gallery.	**1959** Receives another cascade of awards and has exhibitions worldwide.	**1963** Takes up etching. Moore receives Order of Merit from Queen Elizabeth II.	**1972** The Henry Moore Trust is set up. **1974** The Henry Moore Sculpture Centre is opened in Ontario, Canada.	**1982** Henry Moore Centre opens in Leeds. A Moore *Reclining Figure*, carved in 1946, makes $1,000,000 at an auction in New York.
1953 Wins International Sculpture Prize at second São Paulo Biennale.	**1960** Many German towns commission large bronzes by Moore as public sculptures.	**1964** Appointed member of the Arts Council of Great Britain. Reappointed Trustee of National Gallery. **1965** Buys a summer house in Italy. Visits New York.	**1975** Hepworth dies. **1977** The Henry Moore Foundation opens. Moore's grandson Gus is born.	**1983** Moore's health continues to deteriorate. **31 August 1986** Henry Moore dies.

Glossary

Abstraction: an art movement which became influential between 1910 and 1920. Abstract art does not imitate the world around us – it is often impossible to recognise objects, people or places. Wassily Kandinsky (1866-1944) and Piet Mondrian (1872-1944) were both leading Abstract artists.

artefact: any man-made object of historical importance, such as pottery, jewellery or textiles.

avant-garde: describes new, experimental or radical ideas. From the French for vanguard, the first troops in a battle.

Biennale: a prestigious international art exhibition held every two years. Biennales occur in cities around the world, but the most famous one is the Venice Biennale, which first took place in 1895.

Bohemian: describes a person, often an artist or intellectual, who lives in a way that does not follow social conventions.

casting: the process of creating a sculpture by pouring molten metal into a mould.

Classical: describes something from the period of European history which was dominated by the ancient Greek and then Roman civilisations. Classical art usually involved the realistic portrayal of the human figure.

commission: to place an order for something (e.g. a work of art), or a work of art created to order.

conscription: compulsory service in the armed forces.

critic: a person who makes a living by writing about the arts.

Cubism: the name of an art movement based in Paris from about 1907, led by Georges Braque (1882-1963) and Pablo Picasso (1881-1973). The Cubists painted multiple viewpoints of a person or object so all angles were seen at once.

direct carving: the technique of carving directly into stone or wood using a hammer and chisel.

etching: a print on paper made from an engraved metal plate.

exhibition: a public showing of artworks.

Fascism: an extreme right-wing political system where the government holds total power, usually focused around a charismatic leader.

foundry: a place where casting is carried out.

manifesto: a declaration of beliefs.

Modernist: term used to cover all of the art movements of the early 20th century, including Cubism, Surrealism and Abstraction.

Old Masters: the greatest European painters during the period 1500-1800, including Leonardo da Vinci (1452-1519), Michelangelo (1475-1564) and Rembrandt (1606-69).

primitive art: art created by peoples outside the Western, 'developed' world – for example by Native Americans or by African or Oceanic peoples.

relief: a three-dimensional image projected off a flat surface.

Renaissance: from the French word 'rebirth'. Describes the European intellectual and artistic movement which began in 14th-century Italy and was at its height (the High Renaissance) in the 16th century. During the Renaissance, Classical ideas were rediscovered, or 'reborn'.

retrospective: an exhibition showing an artist's development over his or her lifetime.

slag heap: a hillock of waste left by the mining industry.

studio: an artist's workshop.

Surrealism: an intellectual movement that began in the 1920s, which tried to show the life of our unconscious minds and dreams. The Surrealists included artists, writers and film-makers.

unconscious: describes the part of a person's mind that lies outside the conscious mind we use in everyday waking life, such as dreams.

Victorian: the period during the reign of Queen Victoria in Great Britain (1837-1901). At this time, British society was morally strict and traditional, and art was based on the classical style.

Museums and galleries

Works by Moore are exhibited in museums, galleries, streets and squares and towns and gardens all around the world. Some of the ones listed here are devoted solely to Moore, but most have a wide range of other artists' works on display.

Even if you can't visit any of these galleries yourself, you may be able to visit their websites. Gallery websites often show pictures of the artworks they have on display. Some of the websites even offer virtual tours which allow you to wander around and look at different paintings while sitting comfortably in front of your computer!

Most of the international websites detailed below include an option that allows you to view them in English.

EUROPE

Didrichsen Art Museum
Kuusilahdenkuja 1
00340 Helsinki
Finland
www.didrichsenmuseum.fi

The Henry Moore Foundation
Dane Tree House
Perry Green
Much Hadham
Hertfordshire
SG10 6EE
www.henry-moore-fdn.co.uk

Leeds City Art Gallery
The Headrow
Leeds
LS1 3AA
www.leeds.gov.uk/artgallery

Manchester Art Gallery
Mosley Street
Manchester
M2 3JL
www.manchestergalleries.org

**The National Museum
and Gallery of Wales**
Cathays Park
Cardiff
CF10 3NP
Wales
www.nmgw.ac.uk/nmgc

Tate Britain
Millbank
London
SW1P 4RG
www.tate.org.uk

Ulster Museum
Botanic Gardens
Belfast, Northern Ireland
BT9 5AB
www.ulstermuseum.org.uk

Wakefield Art Gallery
Wentworth Terrace
Wakefield
WF1 3QW
www.wakefield.gov.uk/community/
museumsarts/wkgalery.htm

USA

Albright-Knox Art Gallery
1285 Elmwood Avenue
Buffalo
New York 14222-1096
www.albrightknox.org

**Hirshhorn Museum and
Sculpture Garden**
Smithsonian Institution
PO Box 37012
MRC Code 350
Washington, DC 20013-7012
hirshhorn.si.edu

Metropolitan Museum of Art
1000 Fifth Avenue at 82nd Street
New York
New York 10028-0198
www.metmuseum.org

**The Nelson-Atkins Museum
of Art**
4525 Oak Street
Kansas City
Missouri 64111-1873
www.nelson-atkins.org/
sculpture/henrymoore/
henrymoore.htm

REST OF THE WORLD

Art Gallery of New South Wales
Art Gallery Road, The Domain
Sydney, NSW 2000
Australia
www.artgallery.nsw.gov.au

The Art Gallery of Ontario
317 Dundas Street West
Toronto, Ontario M5T 1G4
Canada
www.ago.net

The Hakone Open Air Museum
1121, Ninotaira, Hakone-machi,
Ashigarashimo-gun, Kanagawa
Japan
www.hakone-oam.or.jp

Index